BUSINESS PLAN ON
Catfish Production And Marketing
(A Comprehensive Guide)

Brendan B. Michael

© Brendan B. Michael 2022

All rights reserved. No part of this publication may be reproduced, stored in a retrieval system, or transmitted in any form or by any means, electronic, mechanical, photocopying, recording or otherwise, without the prior written permission of the copyright owner.

ISBN: 9798846481961

Published By:
McBrandon Publishers
(A Div. of McBrandon Business Consulting)
1, Olukoya Street,
Felele Rab,
Ibadan, Nigeria.
Tel.: +2348135830704, +2348030655262, +2349059371424.
E-mail: mcbrandonbc@gmail.com
Website: www.mcbrandon-business-consulting.com.ng

Contents

Contents	3
Title Page	5
Executive Summary	6
Chapter One: Introduction	8
Catfish Business - Current Situation In Nigeria	8
Potential For Success In Ibadan	9
Institutional Framework	9
Chapter Two: Business/Market Analyses	12
The Business	12
Market Analyses	13
Operating Environment	13
Competition	13
Marketing Strategy	14
SWOT Analysis	15
Target Market	16
Market Areas	16
Chapter Three: The Product	18
Fingerlings	18
Juvenile	19
Table-sized	19
Product Prices	19
Breeding/Hatching Cost	20
Cost of Feeding 500,000 Fingerlings And Juvenile For Eight Weeks	20
Chapter Four: Technical Analysis	22
Feeding Plan Analysis	23
Machinery/Equipment Requirements	24
Management and Manpower Analysis	25
Raw Materials Cost Analysis	26
Overhead Cost Analysis	27
Working Capital Analysis	27
Capital Contribution Analysis	28

Analysis of Projected Turnover 30
Unit Cost Analysis 31
Gross Profit Analysis 31
Statement of Cash Flows For Five Years 32

Chapter Five: General Appraisal of The Business 34

LIST OF TABLES
Table 1: Table Showing Product Description And Prices 19
Table 2: Table Showing Cost of Two Sets of Broodstock... 20
Table 3: Table Showing Cost of Feeding 500,000 Fingerlings and... 20
Table 4: Table Showing Cost of Feeding 2,000 Table-sized Catfish... 21
Table 5: Table Showing Feeding Plan For 200,000 Catfish Up To Five Months 23
Table 6: Table Showing Machinery and Equipment Used For Daily Operations 24
Table 7: Table Showing Projected Remuneration for Management/Staff 25
Table 7B: Table Showing Five-year Projected Management/Staff Remuneration 26
Table 8: Table Showing Cost of Raw Materials For The Production and Sale... 26
Table 9: Table Showing Analysis of Overhead Cost For The Production and... 27
Table 10: Table Showing Analysis of Working Capital For The Production and... 27
Table 11: Table Showing Analysis of The Business Capital Contribution 28
Table 12: Table Showing Schedule of Asset Depreciation At 5% Reducing... 29
Table 13: Table Showing Projected Turnover (Collections) for Five Months 30
Table 14: Table showing cost of producing a unit of different sizes of catfish 31
Table 15: Table Showing Analysis of Gross Profit 31
Table 16: Table Showing Statement of Cash Flows For Five Years 32
Table 17: Capital Requirement and Intended Use 35

LIST OF FIGURES
Figure 1: SWOT Analysis for Mybusiness Global Enterprise 16
Figure 2: Developmental Plan For Catfish Production... 23
Figure 3: Pie Chart Showing The Three Different Products We Offer And Their Contributions To Our Annual Turnover 30
Figure 4: Chart Showing Progression of Net Cash Flow For Five Years 32

BUSINESS PLAN ON CATFISH PRODUCTION AND MARKETING

By

Mr. (Your Name) – Managing Director
MYBUSINESS GLOBAL ENTERPRISE
No 1, Mybusiness Drive, Kotilo Village, Via Olorunda-Abaa,
Lagelu LGA, Ibadan.
Telephone: +234 90x xxx xxxx

Prepared By: (NOT NECESSARY IF PREPARED BY SELF)

MCBRANDON BUSINESS CONSULTING
(Marketing/Business Development Consultants)
1, Olukoya Street, Felele Rab, Ibadan, Oyo State, Nigeria.
Tel.: +234 803 065 5262
www.mcbrandon-business-consulting.com.ng

EXECUTIVE SUMMARY

Mybusiness Global Enterprise is a proposed business venture that seeks to leverage commercial catfish farming for potential profit and quick payback period. The business is to be sited on a plot of freehold land at No 1, Mybusiness Drive, Kotilo Village, Via Olorunda-Abaa, Lagelu LGA, Ibadan. The farm's strategic location is one of the many strengths of the business. Lagelu Local Government Area has an estimated population of 180,000. The people in this area are mostly low to medium income earners who have high comparative preference for fish instead of meat.

Second, the FAO estimated Nigeria's annual per capita consumption of fish to be 13.3kg (FAO, November 2017). Using this metric, the estimated daily consumption of fish in the areas surrounding Mybusiness Global Enterprise, including; Iyana-Offa, Olorunda, Lalupon, Lagun, Monatan, Wofun, Oyedeji, Kelebe, Sagbe, Kutayi and environs is **6.5 metric tones.** This was arrived at from a modest estimation of the area's population which currently stands at 180,000. On the other hand, the production capacity of fish farmers in these areas is just **0.6 metric tonnes per day, leaving a production deficit of 5.9 metric tonnes per day. It is clearly evident that the market for catfish in this area is highly unexploited.**

Third, going by the steady progression of the estimated net cash flow, the business can be said to be viable, stable and highly futuristic. It is no less than a cashcow for the business owner, the investors and other stakeholders.

Finally, besides the fact that the operators of the business are experienced fish farmers with a combined professional experience of over ten years in hatchery, fish rearing, catfish nurturing, catfish handling, and catfish marketing; **the business Payback period, for a capital layout of Twelve Million Six Hundred and Thirty-five Thousand Four Hundred Naira (N12,635,400), is as short as three years**. Also, the business can, within five years, produce net cash flow of **N6,206,201.09**.

CHAPTER ONE
INTRODUCTION

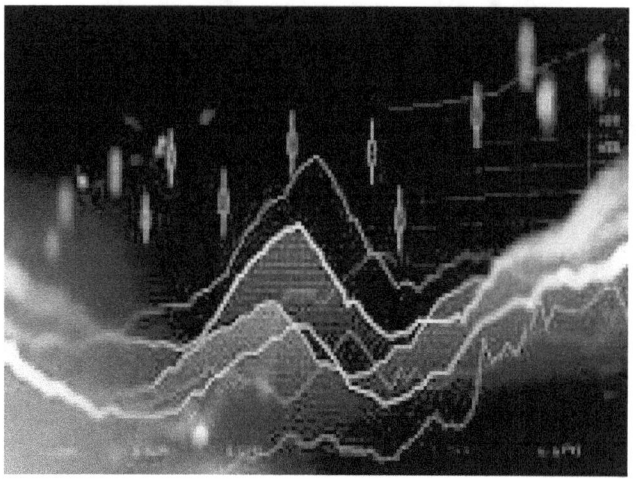

Catfish Business - Current Situation in Nigeria

Fish farming is about the most lucrative business for an average entrepreneur in Nigeria. Apart from the fact that fishing is a major source of livelihood, research has proven that fish represents an important dietary element and one of the few sources of animal protein available to many in Nigeria **(FAO, November, 2017)**.

The annual per capita consumption of fish in Nigeria was estimated to be **13.3 kilograms** in 2013 **(FAO, November, 2017)**. With a population of **160 million Nigerians**, the market potentials for fish farmers is **2.128 billion kilograms** of fish **(2,128,000 metric tonnes)**. Comparing this to the total fishery production, estimated at **1,027,000 tons** in 2015; it is convenient to say that there is marked production deficit of **1,101,000 metric tonnes (51.7%)**.

Potential For Success In Ibadan
Bringing it down to Ibadan, Oyo State, the market coverage area of Mybusiness Global Enterprise; it is not out of place to say there would be a higher fish production deficit. The reason is not far-fetched. Ibadan has smaller water bodies compared to Lagos or other riverine areas of Port Harcourt, Benue and Niger just to mention a few. In other words, the contribution of Ibadan to the pool of total fish production in Nigeria is marginally and comparatively lower; hence, the justification for the setting up and running of this project.

With the above production deficit of **51.7%**, Ibadan requires more fish farmers to meet the consumption needs of the people to the tune of **20,628.3 metric tonnes per annum**. This figure was arrived at by using an estimated population of **3,000,000**.

Apart from the above justification, the social lifestyle of Ibadan is favourable to consumption of Catfish. It is just natural for a beer consumer to demand for a plate of Catfish peppersoup. Both products are complementary.

Additionally, the income pattern of Ibadan people support consumption of more fish than meat. There are more people within the low to medium income bracket and this means that there would be more demand for fish or fish products than there is for meat.

Institutional Framework
Institutionally, there is no specific legislation on aquaculture at the national level as it is not mentioned in the Sea Fisheries Decree and Regulations **(respectively 1992 and 1971)**. However, the Inland Fisheries Decree (1992) makes a single provision empowering the Minister to determine whether the setup of enclosures, such as pens and cages, should be subject to a license fee.

In other words, Nigeria, whether at the national level or at the state levels, has no clear-cut legislation on aquaculture. There are no guidelines or codes of conduct. Fish farms are registered just like any other business without cut-throat bottlenecks.

The provision above has thus created an opportunity for this project to be registered as a Business Name and legal entity with the Corporate Affairs Commission (CAC) on the 20th of February, 2021. It operates under the name: Mybusiness Global Enterprise.

CHAPTER TWO
Business/Market Analyses

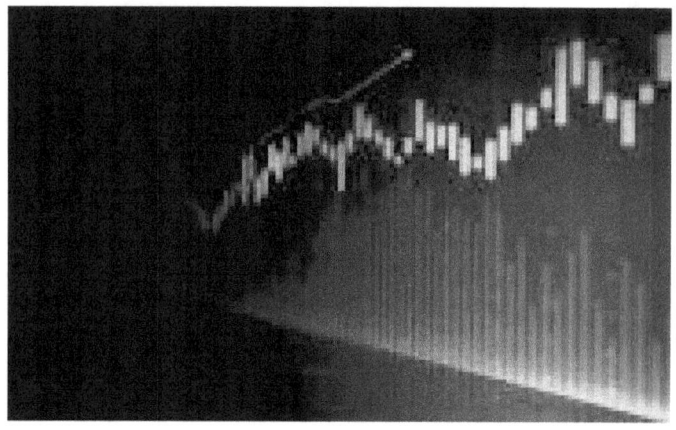

THE BUSINESS

NAME:
Mybusiness Global Enterprise

LOCATION:
No 1, Mybusiness Drive, Kotilo Village, Via Olorunda-Abaa, Lagelu LGA, Ibadan.

VISION
To be the world's busiest catfish marketing company.

MISSION
i. To offer the most customer-friendly prices for all our products;
ii. To offer quality products by investing in up-to-date aquaculture technology;
iii. To factor in highly experienced catfish handlers
iv. To foster effective business-customer communication by fully optimizing the business' digital marketing channels.

MARKET ANALYSIS

OPERATING ENVIRONMENT

The immediate business environment which covers, Iyana-Offa, Olorunda, Lalupon, Lagun, Monatan, Wofun, Oyedeji, Kelebe, Sagbe, Kutayi and others is characterized by Hotels, Guest Houses, Club Houses, Pubs or Joints where catfish is in high demand. There are also hundreds of live Catfish retailers in various markets across the local government area. These retailers sometimes have to, most times, source for catfish from far locations outside the local government area as the current production by the existing farmers in the area is not very little.

Individuals in households also visit the catfish retailers at the various markets in the areas mentioned above as well as within the neighborhoods. This makes it a huge task for the very few Catfish farmers in these areas to meet the growing demand of the retailers and the consumers.

COMPETITION

The number of registered catfish farmers in the market areas mentioned above is about twenty-five. This figure excludes smaller unregistered reseller fish farmers who produce in small tanks and retail to final consumers. The estimated capacity of the fish farms within the area is about **300,000 table-size Catfish or 240,000 kilograms (240 metric tonnes) per annum**, excluding small sized cat fishes (Fingerlings and Juvenile). **This gives an average daily production capacity of 657 kilograms (0.66 metric tones).**

The production capacity of all the players (fish farmers) within the market area does not match the consumption need of over **180,000** population who currently consume up to **2,394,000 kilograms (or 2,394 metric tonnes)** of catfish per annum and by contraction, **6,558 kilograms (6.5 metric tonnes)** per day.

It is therefore evident from the above estimation that the market still has far-reaching opportunities for catfish farmers who are still considering whether to go into production and marketing of catfish. As it stands right now, competition among the existing catfish farmers in the area is still healthy being that there is production deficit of **5,901 kilograms (5.9 metric tonnes)** per day

MARKETING STRATEGY
We are living in the era of social media and digital marketing. One strategy we would not but adopt for the promotion of our products to targeted customers within the market area and Ibadan at large; shall be, to leverage the benefits of digital marketing by creating various channels like Facebook, Blog, Instagram. We would not just end there, we shall optimize these channels for higher conversion.

Part of our strategies also is to deliver our products directly to fish sellers at their places of business. This may initially increase running cost, but in the long run, the business will take advantage of economies of scale when customer base increases.

The business shall run price penetrating strategy, allowing price reduction of about 10% without reducing the value we offer our customers. This is in a bid to encourage resellers to buy more of our products and improve sales.

Finally, we shall maintain optimum quality level by applying the principle of Total Quality Management. It begins with hatching. We ensure that the right fish is used for fertilization. The female fish must be healthy and its eggs must be of high quality too. The spermatozoa of the male catfish used for fertilization must be very healthy. The feeds, the water, the aeration, the tanks (plastic and concrete), the harvest equipment, the fish handling equipment, the disinfectant, the injectibles and other equipment must all meet high quality standards. This helps us to produce healthy fries, fingerlings, juveniles and of course, Table-sized catfish. One of the ways we know our products are healthy is when their weights are right.

SWOT ANALYSIS FOR MYBUSINESS GLOBAL ENTERPRISE
There is no business that does not have its unique **Strengths** and **Weaknesses** or that is not confronted with **Opportunities** and **Threats** from the external environment. Therefore, the SWOT Analysis of Mybusiness Global Enterprise has been conducted and represented in the Pie Chart below:

Figure 1: SWOT Analysis for Mybusiness Global Enterprise

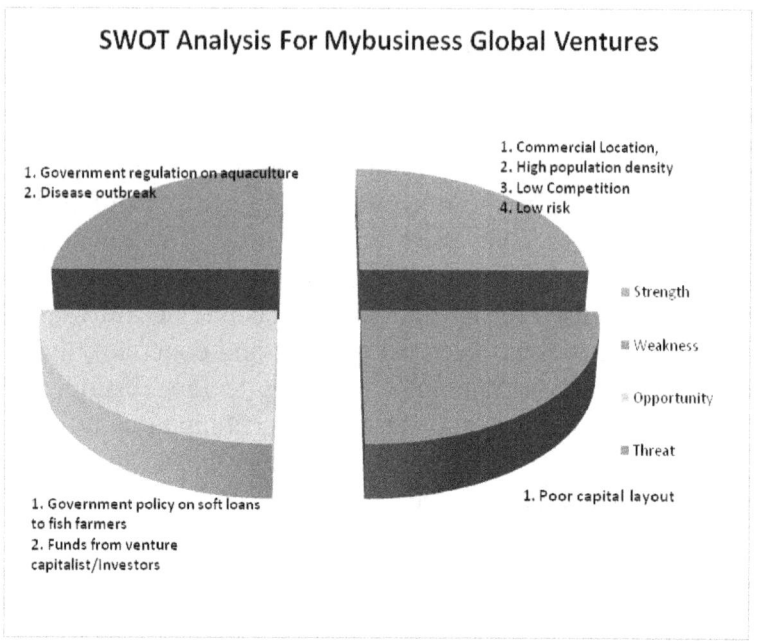

TARGET MARKET
The following are the target markets of the business:
a. Small catfish farmers
b. Catfish resellers scattered around marketplaces and other locations within the market area;
c. Processed catfish sellers (E.g., Hoteliers, Guest House Operators, Joints/Pubs Operators, etc;
d. Consumers.

MARKET AREAS
Iyana-Offa, Olorunda, Lalupon, Lagun, Monatan, Wofun, Oyedeji, Kelebe, Sagbe, Kutayi and environs.

Business/Market Analysis 17

CHAPTER THREE
THE PRODUCT

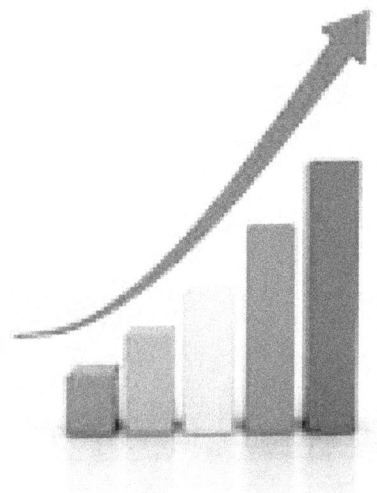

Mybusiness Global Enterprise is planning to go into the production and marketing of Catfish and its target market area (at large) is Ibadan. For efficiency and effectiveness, the business shall focus on the production and marketing of: **A. Fingerlings B. Juvenile C. Table-sized Catfish**

Fingerlings
These are young catfish not more than 5 weeks old after they might have been successfully hatched. The farm shall construct 4 plastic ponds measuring 75cm x 75cm x 105cm in length, breadth and height

The Product

respectively. These ponds shall have the capacity to contain up to Two Million fingerlings. However, as a result of the rather lean capital layout, the farm shall initially, run at 50% capacity. Considering a 50% probability of success, 50% of the successful catfish (250,000) shall be sold as Fingerlings at N5 each. The remaining 250,000 shall be allowed to grow to become Juvenile and Table-sized catfish. From the remaining 250,000, 245,000 shall be sold as Juvenile at N15 each and the remaining 5,000 shall be allowed to grow into Table-sized catfish and sold for N600.

Juvenile
These are catfish between age 6 weeks and 7 weeks. They shall form 49% of the business' inventory with a 46.37% contribution into the business' profit.

Table-sized Catfish
These are catfish that are allowed to grow up to between 5 months and 6 months. Their average weight shall range between 1kg and 1.5kg. They shall form 1% of the business' inventory with a 37.85% contribution into the business' profit. The business shall construct 7 concrete ponds measuring 6ft width x 12ft length x 4ft height to contain the planned production of 5,000 Table-sized catfish.

PRODUCT PRICES
Table 1: Table Showing Product Description And Prices

PRODUCT NAME	DISCOUNTED UNIT PRICE (RESELLER)	DISCOUNTED UNIT PRICE (END USERS)
Fingerlings (4-5 weeks old)	N5.00	N8.00
Juvenile (6-7 weeks old)	N15.00	N20.00
Table-sized Catfish (1kg)	N600.00	650.00

Breeding/Hatching Cost Analysis

The farm shall operate at 50% capacity producing 500,000 catfish, including Fingerlings, Juvenile and Table-sized catfish. To produce this much, we shall use four broodstock (2 male and 2 female) per session of breeding. The session shall be repeated every five months. For details of the breeding cost, see the analysis below:

Cost of Two Sets of Broodstock (Male and Female) Used For Breeding

Eggs from the female catfish are spawned (stripped) and mixed or fertilized in a clean bowl with spermatozoa collected from the male catfish and in about 36 hours, the eggs are hatched and are become living fries (Note: Most times, the process has to be repeated twice to obtain the desired results. Hence the need to make provision for additional set of broodstock.

Table 2: Table Showing Cost of Two Sets of Broodstock Catfish (Male and Female) Used For Breeding

DESCRIPTION	COST AT FIRST TRY	COST AT SECOND TRY
2 Male Broodstock Catfish weighing about 4 kilo	24,000.00	48,000.00
2 Female Broodstock Catfish weighing about 3 kilo	15,000.00	30,000.00
TOTAL		78,000.00

Cost of Feeding 500,000 Fingerlings and Juvenile For 8 Weeks

Coppen's Feeds shall be used to feed our fingerlings. The product has been proven and tested by Catfish farmers in this area. It comes in different variants depending on the age of the fish

Table 3: Table Showing Cost of Feeding 500,000 Fingerlings and Juvenile For 8 Weeks

DESCRIPTION	VARIANTS	QUANTITY (KILO)	AMOUNT/KILO	COST
Cost of Feeding 500,000 Fingerlings from age 1 to 2 weeks	0.2mm	10	2,500.00	25,000.00
Cost of Feeding 500,000 Fingerlings from age 3 to 4 weeks	0.5mm	10	2,500.00	25,000.00
Cost of Feeding 500,000 Fingerlings and Juvenile from age 5 weeks to 6 weeks	1mm	140	1,500.00	210,000.00
Cost of Feeding 245,000 Juvenile from age 7 weeks to 8 weeks	2mm	1,029	1,300.00	1,337,700.00
TOTAL				1,597,700.00

Table 4: Table Showing Cost of Feeding 5,000 Table-sized Catfish For Twelve Weeks (From The 9th Week After Hatching)

DESCRIPTION	VARIANTS	QUANTITY (KILO)	AMOUNT/KILO	COST
Cost of Feeding 5,000 Table-sized Catfish (Age 9 weeks to 10 weeks)	5mm	700	454.00	317,800.00
Cost of Feeding 5,000 Table-sized Catfish (Age 11 weeks to 12 weeks)	7mm	1,050	454.00	476,700.00
Cost of Feeding 5,000 Table-sized Catfish (Age 13 weeks to 16 weeks)	7mm	1,575	454.00	715,050.00
Cost of Feeding 5,000 Table-sized Catfish (Age 17 weeks to 20 weeks)	8mm (Pellet Feed)	1,000	336.00	336,000.00
TOTAL				1,845,550.00

CHAPTER FOUR

TECHNICAL ANALYSES

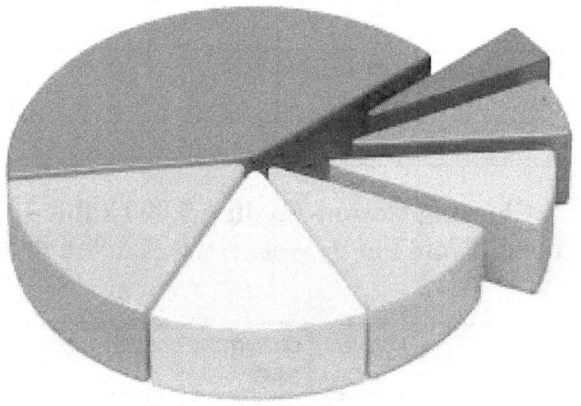

    The farm shall operate both hatchery and adult catfish rearing. Construction of 4 plastic ponds measuring 75cm x 75cm x 105cm in length, breadth and height respectively shall be done. These are needed for breeding/hatching as well as for nurturing the Fingerlings and the Juvenile. These tanks shall be raised a little bit above the floor in order to facilitate cleaning of the tanks and siphoning of fries. The four tanks shall be nurseries for the fries, the fingerlings and the juvenile as they grow older.

At about eight weeks after hatching, the catfish shall be ready for transportation to a bigger concrete pond. There shall be seven concrete ponds measuring 6ft width x 12ft length x 4ft height constructed to accommodate the catfish as they grow older.

Figure 2: Developmental Plan For Catfish Production At Mybusiness Global Enterprise t was self-sustaining.

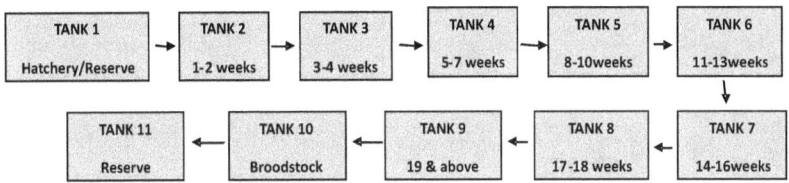

Feeding Plan Analysis
The following feeding plan shall be adopted by Mybusiness Global Enterprise. This plan applies only to not more than 500,000 catfish

Table 5: Table Showing Feeding Plan For 500,000 Catfish Up To Five Months

Catfish Age	No of Catfish	Feed Type/Brand	Feed Quality	Kilo (Feed)	Quantity of Feed
0-2 weeks	500,000	Coppen	0.2mm	10	712.5grammes/Day
3-4 weeks	500,000	Coppen	0.5mm	10	712.5grammes/Day
5-6 weeks	500,000	Coppen	1mm	140	10kilo/Day
7-8 weeks	500,000	Coppen	2mm	1,050	75kilo/Day
9-10 weeks	5,000	Coppen	5mm	1,400	100kilo/Day
11-12 weeks	5,000	Coppen	7mm	2,625	187.5Kilo/Day
13-16 weeks	5,000	Coppen	7mm	2,625	93.75Kilo/Day
17-20 weeks	5,000	Pellet	8mm	2,000	71.5Kilo/Day

Machinery/Equipment Requirements

For effective and efficient production of catfish at Mybusiness Global Enterprise, the following machineries or equipments shall be used:

Table 6: Table Showing Machinery and Equipment Required For Daily Operations At Mybusiness Global Enterprise

Description	Type	Units	Use
Equipment			
Tank	Plastic and Concrete	11	For breeding and rearing Catfish (Refer To Figure 2)
Dip Nets	Different mesh sizes	4	For easy retrieval/collection of Catfish
Graders		2	For grading out jumpers (jumpy catfish) or shooters (catfish that outgrow others)
Buckets & Plastic Tubs		10	For holding brood fish and for anaesthetics use (for calming the fish during the breeding process)
Siphons		4	For siphoning off waste from the bottom of the tank and for moving fries out of the tank
Others			
Overhead Water Tanks		6	For regular supply of clean water to the fish tanks and for use within the farm
Machinery			
Pumping Machine	2 HP	1	For pumping water into the water tanks for onward supply to the fish tanks

Management and Manpower Analysis

The business shall operate with the capacity to produce over 10,000 adult catfish or 2 million fingerlings per time. However, to accommodate possible lean capital layout, it shall operate at a 50% capacity employing one management personnel and three junior staff members including: one Managing Director as the Chief Executive and Head of Business Operations and Three Farm Attendants who take care of the feeding of the fish, cleaning of equipment and the environment, changing of water as and when due and other general duties on a daily basis. The total actual cost of labour is as follows:

Management and Manpower Analysis

The business shall operate with the capacity to produce over 10,000 adult catfish or 2 million fingerlings per time. However, to accommodate possible lean capital layout, it shall operate at a 50% capacity employing one management personnel and three junior staff members including: one Managing Director as the Chief Executive and Head of Business Operations and Three Farm Attendants who take care of the feeding of the fish, cleaning of equipment and the environment, changing of water as and when due and other general duties on a daily basis. The total actual cost of labour is as follows:

Table 7: Table Showing Projected Remuneration for Management/Staff of Mybusiness Global Enterprise

POST	UNIT REQUIRED	ROLE	PROJECTED MONTHLY REMUNERATION	PROJECTED ANNUAL REMUNERATION
Managing Director	1	Heads business operations and other executive functions including business development, marketing, third party and customer relations management and other managerial roles. He also acts as the farm's Manager/Supervisor	150,000.00	1,800,000.00
Farm Attendants	3	Feeding of the fish, cleaning of equipment and the environment, changing of water as and when due and other general duties.	105,000	1,260,000.00
TOTAL	4		255,000.00	3,060,000.00

Provision for Annual Salary increase is allowed at 5% per annum. The projection for five years will then appear as follows:

Table 7B: Table Showing Five-year Projected Management/Staff Remuneration

Year	1	2	3	4	5
Staff Remuneration (₦)	3,060,000.00	3,213,000	3,373,650	3,542,332.50	3,719,449.13

RAW MATERIALS COST ANALYSIS

The analysis below shows the cost of materials for the production and sale of 250,000 Fingerlings, 245,000 Juveniles and 5,000 Table-sized Catfish within the period of five months:

Table 8: Table Showing Cost of Raw Materials For The Production and Sale of 250,000 Fingerlings, 245,000 Juveniles and 5,000 Table-sized Catfish Within The Period of Five Months

S/N	RAW MATERIALS NAME	COST PER KILO/UNIT	UNIT REQUIRED (KILO)	COST	TOTAL COST
1	Hatching (Fertilization) (Refer to Table 1)				78,000.00
2	Feeds				
	Coppen (0.2mm)	2,500.00	10	25,000.00	
	Coppen (0.5mm)	2,500.00	10	25,000.00	
	Coppen (1mm)	1,500.00	140	210,000.00	
	Coppen (2mm)	1,300.00	1,050	1,365,000.00	
	Coppen (5mm)	454.00	1,400	635,600.00	
	Coppen (7mm)	454.00	5,250	2,383,500.00	
	Pellet (8mm)	336.00	2,000	672,000.00	
	SUB-TOTAL				5,316,100.00
3	Injectibles				
	Ovalline	6,000.00	1	6,000.00	
	N Saline Water	200.00	1	200.00	
	Syringe	100.00	1 Pack	100.00	
	SUB-TOTAL				6,300.00
4	Disinfectants/Cleaning Agents				
	Izal	400.00	10	4,000.00	
	Detergents	100	10	1,000.00	
	SUB-TOTAL				5,000.00
	TOTAL				5,405,400.00

OVERHEAD COST ANALYSIS

The analysis below shows the estimated cost of overheads required for the production and sale of 250,000 Fingerlings, 245,000 Juveniles and 5,000 Table-sized Catfish within the period of five months:

Table 9: Table Showing Analysis of Overhead Cost For The Production and Sale of 250,000 Fingerlings, 245,000 Juveniles and 5,000 Table-sized Catfish Within The Period of Five Months

S/N	Description	Cost
1	Indirect Labour Cost/Wage (Including: Gardening, Plumbing, Electrical Repairs and other related services) at N10,000 per month	50,000.00
2	Electricity Bill at N6,000 per month	30,000.00
3	Selling/Promotional Cost (Banners, Telephone Calls, Transportation, Digital Marketing, Complimentary Cards and Gifts) at N10,000 per month	50,000.00
	TOTAL	130,000.00

WORKING CAPITAL ANALYSIS

The working capital for the business for a period of five months is analyzed as follows:

Table 10: Table Showing Analysis of Working Capital For The Production and Sale of 250,000 Fingerlings, 245,000 Juveniles and 5,000 Table-sized Catfish Within The Period of Five Months

S/N	Description	Cost
1	Raw Materials (Refer To Table 8)	5,405,400.00
2	Overhead Cost (Refer To Table 9)	130,000.00
	TOTAL	5,535,400.00

NOTE: CALCULATION OF ANNUAL WORKING CAPITAL AND AVERAGE MONTHLY WORKING CAPITAL: From the above total, the annual working capital can be calculated by multiplying N5,535,400 by 2.4. That is, **N13,284,960.00**. The average monthly working capital can therefore be arrived at by dividing N5,535,400 by 5. That is, **N1,107,080.00.**.

CAPITAL STRUCTURE AND CONTRIBUTION ANALYSIS

The table below analyzes the capital structure/requirements and their sources:

Table 11: Table Showing Analysis of The Business Capital Contribution

S/N	Description	Owner's Equity	Loan	Overdraft	Total
1	Land	1,200,000	-	-	1,200,000.00
2	Plastic Tanks (4 Units at N20,000 each)	-	80,000.00	-	80,000.00
3	Construction of 7 Concrete Tanks	-	3,000,000.00	-	3,000,000.00
4	Plumbing Fixtures (Including Borehole, Overhead Tanks (6 Units), Water Pipes and Pumping Machine)	-	1,100,000.00	-	1,100,000.00
5	Working Capital	-	13,284,960.00	-	13,284,960.00
6	3.5 KVA Thermocool Generator	-	170,000.00	-	170,000.00
7	Tokunbo Pickup Van (For Marketing and Sales)	-	1,500,000.00	-	1,500,000.00
	TOTAL	1,200,000.00	19,134,960.00	-	20,334,960.00

PROVISION FOR DEPRECIATION

Find below the schedule of provision for fixed assets depreciation. Depreciation is calculated at 5% reducing balance per annum:

Table 12: Table Showing Schedule of Asset Depreciation At 5% Reducing Balance Per Annum

Description	Plastic Tanks	Concrete Tanks	Plumbing Fixtures	Pickup Van	Gen.	TOTAL
Cost	80,000.00	3,000,000.00	1,100,000.00	1,500,000.00	170,000.00	5,850,000.00
Year 1 Depreciation	4,000.00	150,000.00	55,000.00	75,000.00	8,500.00	292,500.00
Value After Year 1	76,000.00	2,850,000.00	1,045,000.00	1,425,000.00	161,500.00	5,557,500.00
Year 2 Depreciation	3,800.00	142,500.00	52,250.00	71,250.00	8,075.00	277,875.00
Value After Year 2	72,200.00	2,707,500.00	992,750.00	1,353,750.00	153,425.00	5,279,625.00
Year 3 Depreciation	3,610.00	135,375.00	49,637.50	67,687.50	7,671.25	263,981.25
Value After Year 3	68,590.00	2,527,125.00	943,112.50	1,286,062.50	145,803.75	4,970,693.75
Year 4 Depreciation	3,429.50	126,356.25	47,155.63	64,303.13	7,290.19	248,534.70
\Value After Year 4	65,160.50	2,400,768.75	895,956.87	1,221,759.38	138,513.56	4,722,159.06
Year 5 Depreciation	3,258.03	120,038.44	44,797.84	61,087.97	6,925.68	236,107.96
Value After Year 5	61,902.47	2,280,730.31	851,159.03	1,160,671.41	131,587.88	4,486,051.10

ANALYSIS OF PROJECTED TURNOVER (COLLECTIONS)

The business shall run about 2.4 production cycle in a year. This is in a bid to minimize cost of feeding. Every five months, 500,000 catfish shall be produced. This includes 250,000 Fingerlings which shall be sold at N5 each, 245,000 Juveniles to be sold at N15 each and the remaining 5,000 catfish are to be nurtured to maturity (19-20 weeks) and shall be sold at N600 each.

The above sales are tabulated as follows:

Table 13: Table Showing Projected Turnover (Collections) for Five Months

S/N	Description	Unit	Amount Per Unit (₦)	Amount (₦)
1	Fingerlings	250,000	5	1,250,000.00
2	Juvenile	245,000	15	3,675,000.00
3	Table-sized	5,000	600	3,000,000.00
TOTAL				7,925,000.00

NOTE: CALCULATION OF PROJECTED ANNUAL TURNOVER AND AVERAGE MONTHLY TURNOVER: From the above total, the annual collections from customers can be calculated by multiplying N7,925,000 by 2.4. That is, **N19,020,000.00**. The average monthly collections can therefore be arrived at by dividing N19,020,000 by 12. That is, **N1,585,000.00**

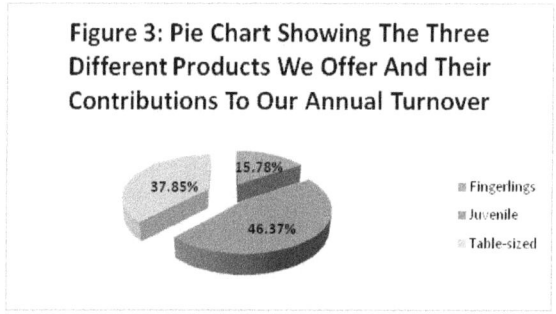

Figure 3: Pie Chart Showing The Three Different Products We Offer And Their Contributions To Our Annual Turnover

UNIT COST ANALYSIS
Table 14: Table showing cost of producing a unit of different sizes of catfish

TOTAL UNITS (PA)	COST OF LABOUR (PA) @ 15.78%, 46.37% and 37.85% respectively.	WORKING CAPITAL (PA) @ 15.77%, 46.37% and 37.86% respectively.	TOTAL COST	COST PER UNIT
600,000 Units of Fingerlings	482,868.00	2,095,038.19	2,577,906.19	4.29
588,000 Units of Juvenile	1,418,922.00	6,160,235.95	7,579,157.95	12.89
12,000 Units of Table-sized Catfish	1,158,210.00	5,029,685.86	6,187,895.86	515.66
TOTAL	3,060,000.00	13,284,960.00	16,344,960.00	

GROSS PROFIT ANALYSIS
Table 15: Table Showing Analysis of Gross Profit

DESCRIPTION	UNIT COST	UNIT PRICE	PROFIT PER UNIT	PERCENTAGE PROFIT
Fingerlings	4.29	5.00	0.71	16.55
Juvenile	12.89	15.00	2.11	16.36
Table-sized Catfish	515.66	600.00	84.34	16.35
AVERAGE				16.42

Note: The above table shows that the break-even prices for the production of a unit each of Fingerling, Juvenile and Table-sized Catfish are N4.29, N12.89 and N515.66. In other words, selling below these prices will amount to a loss to the business. Also, each of the products has an average of 16.42% gross profit margin if sold at N5, N15 and N600 respectively

STATEMENT OF CASH FLOWS FOR FIVE YEARS

The Statement of Cash Flows for Mybusiness Global Enterprise is calculated thus:

Table 16: Table Showing Mybusiness Global Enterprise Statement of Cash Flows For Five Years

PARTICULARS	Year 0	Year 1	Year 2	Year 3	Year 4	Year 5
Receipts						
Opening Balance	0.00	(5,850,000.00)	(3,467,460.00)	(1,070,295.00)	1,340,763.75	3,767,269.05
Collections From Customers (Refer To Table 15 – Note)	0.00	19,020,000.00	19,020,000.00	19,020,000.00	19,020,000.00	19,020,000.00
Total Cash Available	0.00	13,170,000.00	15,552,540.00	17,949,705.00	20,360,763.75	22,787,269.05
Payments						
Working Capital (Refer To Table 10 under Note)	0.00	(13,284,960.00)	(13,284,960.00)	(13,284,960.00)	(13,284,960.00)	(13,284,960.00)
Fixed Capital (Refer To Table 12)	(5,850,000.00)	0.00	0.00	0.00	0.00	0.00
Labour Cost	0.00	(3,060,000.00)	(3,060,000.00)	(3,060,000.00)	(3,060,000.00)	(3,060,000.00)
Depreciation	0.00	(292,500.00)	(277,875.00)	(263,981.25)	(248,534.70)	(236,107.96)
Total Projected Payments	(5,850,000.00)	(16,637,460.00)	(16,622,835.00)	(16,608,941.25)	(16,593,494.70)	(16,581,067.96)
Net Cash Flows	(5,850,000.00)	(3,467,460.00)	(1,070,295.00)	1,340,763.75	3,767,269.05	6,206,201.09

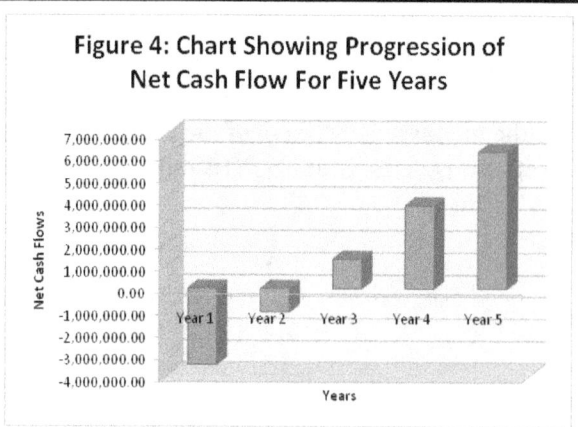

Figure 4: Chart Showing Progression of Net Cash Flow For Five Years

CHAPTER FIVE

GENERAL APPRAISAL

The following metrics were obtained from this business plan and they form part of the conviction that the business is both feasible and viable:

A. Production capacity of the very few Catfish farmers within the market area comprising, Iyana-Offa, Olorunda, Lalupon, Lagun, Monatan, Wofun, Oyedeji, Kelebe, Sagbe, Kutayi and environs is very low. This is obviously why there is production deficit of up to **5.9 metric tonnes** of catfish per day. The market is still unexploited;

B. At about 50% capacity utilization, the business can still produce net cash flow of **N6,206,201.09** in just five years given a capital layout of **N12,635,400.00 (Refer To Table 17)**. At full capacity, the result will be astronomical;

C. The business is viable, stable and highly futuristic. This is because it maintains a sustainable estimated net cash flow progression.

D. The Payback Period of the business is approximately three years – a reasonable period for recouping investment.

Finally, with the right capacity and capital layout, the business can produce even far greater results. Having considered a possible shortage of fund and the importance of this project, the lowest possible capital layout and its intended use have been proposed as follows:

Table 17: Capital Requirement and Intended Use

S/N	Details of Loan Application	Amount Required
1	Pick-up Van For Sales and Marketing Purpose	1,500,000.00
2	Plastic Tanks (4 Units at N20,000 each)	80,000.00
3	Construction of 7 Concrete Tanks	3,000,000.00
4	Plumbing Fixtures (Including Borehole, Overhead Tanks (6 Units), Water Pipes and Pumping Machine)	1,100,000.00
5	Generator	170,000.00
6	Working Capital Requirement (For the first five months of production)	5,535,400.00
7	Labour Cost (For the first five months of production)	1,250,000.00
	Total Loan Required	**12,635,400.00**

NOTE